LOS ANGELES

THE CITY AT A GLANCE

KU-156-723

Echo Park
Check out the increasingly fashionable cafés and shops around Alvarado Street and W Sunset Boulevard.

Dodger Stadium
One of America's most pleasant ballparks, once home to the Latino community of Chavez Ravine, which was forced out to make way for the LA Dodgers' new home.
1000 Elysian Park Avenue, T 323 224 2966

777 Tower
This 52-story white-steel and glass tower, designed by Cesar Pelli & Associates, is just distinctive enough to stand out from the Downtown crowd.
777 S Figueroa Street

Walt Disney Concert Hall
Buried among the skyscrapers, Frank Gehry's home for the Los Angeles Philarmonic is an absolute must-see, inside and out.
See p014

Caltrans HQ
For some, this building suggests the aliens have landed Downtown; for the Pritzker jury, Thom Mayne's transport HQ represents the rootless nature of the city.
See p011

Little Tokyo
Order great sushi and sashimi at restaurant and gallery R-23 (T 213 687 7178) and shop for top pots at Little Tokyo Clayworks (see p085).

San Gabriel Mountains
In winter, Angelenos like to retreat to the San Gabriels for a spot of snowboarding. Summer can see search and rescue picking up hikers with no way down from a mountain ledge.

INTRODUCTION
THE CHANGING FACE OF THE URBAN SCENE

It's long been easy to knock LA. Even Raymond Chandler, the city's own laureate, called it a 'big hard-boiled city, with no more personality than a paper cup' and he lambasted the 'drab anonymity of a thousand shabby lives' lived out there. And that was in the good times. After a decade of race riots, mudslides and tech stock flameouts, Los Angeles started the 21st century in a poor way. But a slow bounce back began with the new millennium. House prices have gone through the roof, tourism is at record post-9/11 levels, and the major media have snapped up hot LA online ideas such as MySpace.com and Weblogs Inc. The economic revival has seen previously overlooked neighbourhoods, such as Silver Lake and Venice, become super-desirable addresses. Meanwhile, the city's re-found confidence is to be found knocking back mojitos in the design-led eateries, bars and hotels that pepper the city in a high-priced arc from the Patina restaurant (see p058) to the Nacional (see p062) in newly buzzing Hollywood.

The city of Eames, Neutra and 'Googie' has always had few equals in its appreciation of challenging design, and it shows in the rows of stores stocking Danish mid-century sideboards and the star status given to the people creating the look of today's LA, from Kelly Wearstler to Thom Mayne and, of course, Frank Gehry. The city is again a bellwether for the kind of high-end design that, one day, will be the backdrop to all our leisure hours.

ESSENTIAL INFO
FACTS, FIGURES AND USEFUL ADDRESSES

TOURIST OFFICE
Hollywood Information Center
6801 Hollywood Boulevard
T 323 467 6412
www.seemyla.com

TRANSPORT
Car hire
Avis, T 310 342 9200
Hertz, T 310 568 5100
Metro
T 213 922 6000
www.metro.net
Taxis
Limo Taxi, T 310 845 1234
Yellow Cab, T 310 808 1000

EMERGENCY SERVICES
Emergencies
T 911
Police (non-emergencies)
Central Community Police Station
251 East Sixth Street
T 213 485 3294
24-hour pharmacy
Savon
2530 Glendale Boulevard
T 323 666 1285

CONSULATES
British Consulate
Suite 1200
11766 Wilshire Boulevard
T 310 481 0031
www.britainusa.com

MONEY
American Express
8493 W 3rd Street/
N La Cienega Boulevard
T 310 659 1682
www10.americanexpress.com

POSTAL SERVICES
Post Office
300 N Los Angeles Street
T 800 275 8777
Shipping
UPS
T 800 742 5877
www.ups.com

BOOKS
Building the Getty by Richard Meier
(University of California Press)
**Deco Landmarks: Art Deco Gems
of Los Angeles** by Arnold Schwartzman
and Bevis Hillier (Chronicle Books)
John Lautner, Architect by Frank Escher
(Princeton Architectural Press)

WEBSITES
Architecture/Design
www.franklloydwright.org
www.pritzkerprize.com/gehry.htm
Art
www.getty.edu
www.lacma.org
www.moca.org
Newspapers
www.latimes.com
www.laweekly.com

COST OF LIVING
**Taxi from LAX
to Downtown**
€73.50
Cappuccino
€2
Packet of cigarettes
€3.50
Daily newspaper
€0.45
Bottle of champagne
€105

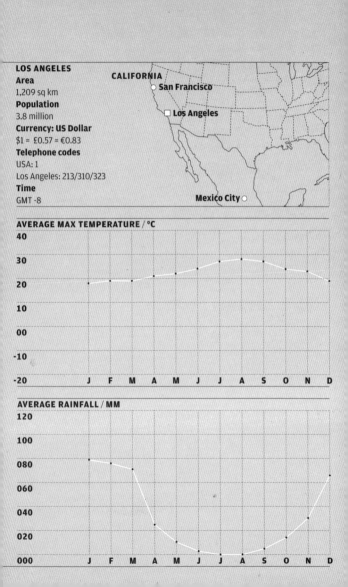

LOS ANGELES
Area
1,209 sq km
Population
3.8 million
Currency: US Dollar
$1 = £0.57 = €0.83
Telephone codes
USA: 1
Los Angeles: 213/310/323
Time
GMT -8

CALIFORNIA
○ San Francisco
□ Los Angeles
Mexico City ○

AVERAGE MAX TEMPERATURE / °C

	J	F	M	A	M	J	J	A	S	O	N	D

40
30
20
10
00
-10
-20

AVERAGE RAINFALL / MM

120
100
080
060
040
020
000

J F M A M J J A S O N D

NEIGHBOURHOODS
THE AREAS YOU NEED TO KNOW AND WHY

To help you navigate the city, we've chosen the most interesting districts (see the map inside the back cover) and underlined featured venues in colour, according to their location (see below); those venues that are outside these areas are not coloured.

WEST HOLLYWOOD AND MIDTOWN
A contender for the heart of the western side of the city, WeHo is home to LA's gay district and, not coincidentally, to some of its most sumptuous designer shopping, whether it be Hollywood regency or mid-century modern. There are many places to eat and be seen, in addition to the ever-growing list of hip hotels and unmissable icons, such as Chateau Marmont (see p020).

SANTA MONICA, VENICE AND CULVER CITY
These are three neighbouring cities, each at different levels of development. Santa Monica has always been affluent and liberal, but several recently opened hotels have given it a new edge. Artsy Venice's Abbot Kinney Boulevard has long been rattling to the sound of the gentrifiers' hammers in a process that is very nearly complete; while Culver City's furniture stores and galleries have transformed it from a forgettable suburb to a must-see.

BEVERLY HILLS AND WESTWOOD
Money has almost bleached out any character, but Beverly Hills retains enough industry magic in hidden places, such as The Fountain Coffee Room at The Beverly Hills Hotel (see p042), to make it worth a visit. Further west, the Getty Center's white bauhaus building, designed by Richard Meier, (see p076) has by itself dragged Westwood onto the visitor's map.

HOLLYWOOD
While Hollywood Boulevard remains a strip of tourist tat, the side streets have been transformed by the arrival of a series of new restaurants and clubs – usually owned by movie money, and designed by the likes of Dodd Mitchell or Thomas Schoos. North Cahuenga Boulevard is the epicentre of new Hollywood, where bars have been opening faster than a valet can park your Bentley Continental.

LOS FELIZ AND SILVER LAKE
Recently dubbed the coolest of LA's neighbourhoods by *Vanity Fair*, Silver Lake is a largely residential area, but with the advantage that many of the houses were designed by the likes of Richard Neutra, Rudolf M Schindler or John Lautner. It has avoided chain-stores, and is instead home to a clutch of boutiques, cafés, bars and restaurants concentrated on Vermont Avenue and Silver Lake Boulevard.

DOWNTOWN
Once was a time when after-hours Downtown seemed only for the homeless. There was little in the way of culture to bring anyone in from the west. Even after years of investment and several claims of a renaissance, it can still feel like a ghost town. Yet the area's quiet canyons play host to two of the most dazzling modern buildings in America: the Caltrans District 7 Headquarters (see p010) and the Walt Disney Concert Hall (see p014).

LANDMARKS
THE SHAPE OF THE CITY SKYLINE

Not for nothing have some of the most acclaimed film treatments of LA, from *Short Cuts* and *Pulp Fiction* to *Magnolia* and *Crash*, been patchwork films that capture the city only by using multiple interwoven storylines. They echo the alienating sprawl of the megalopolis and reveal its potential to put the fear of god into first-time visitors. In fact, thanks to the mountains to the north, the sea to the west and the well-signposted boulevards and freeways, it is a surprisingly easy city to negotiate – especially if you miss out the two-thirds of it that holds little allure to the traveller.

But you must, must, have a car. The main areas to explore can be found in an arc that runs north-west from Downtown, through Hollywood to Venice. The largely Latino East LA and the Valley to the north of the mountains have individual pockets of interest, but the visitor is unlikely to have time to seek them out. The big social-ising areas are in Hollywood and West Hollywood, although there is also plenty to be done by the sea. There are many shopping areas, but pricey design can be found in spades just below West Hollywood in Midtown. You go to Silver Lake for hip boutiques and for its SoCal (Southern Californian) modern architecture and Downtown for more formal pleasures, including Frank Gehry's Walt Disney Concert Hall (see p014) and the fabulous MOCA (250 S Grand Avenue, T 213 626 6222).

For all addresses, see Resources.

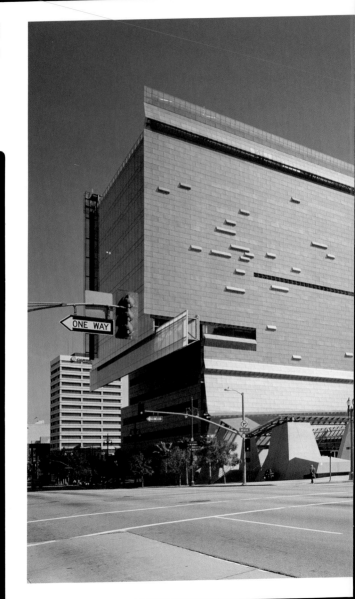

Caltrans District 7 Headquarters

The building that helped Thom Mayne bring the Pritzker Prize back to America in 2005, for the first time in 14 years, the Caltrans has been likened by some city detractors to the Death Star. It certainly is imposing; a matt grey steel hulk of a building taking up a whole city block. But, it is made graceful by the many perforations in its metal skin, the folds and openings of which break up the building's lines while Keith Sonnier's neon installation – attached to the building itself and suggestive of brake lights on an LA freeway – adds some much-needed levity. If you stand on the north-west corner of the junction of Broadway and 1st Street you can see the Walt Disney Concert Hall (see p014) and the Caltrans HQ at the same time.
100 S Main Street

Norms Restaurant

Everyone has their own favourite 'Googie', a nickname for the coffee shop modern style of architecture introduced by John Lautner. Pann's in Inglewood (T 310 670 1441) is often cited as the best example, but it's a long way from anywhere, sited in a *Pulp Fiction* suburb. Norms is in the heart of West Hollywood, but doesn't feel like a tourist attraction or an architecture museum. It's a living structure, a little shabby at the edges and in need of new ceiling tiles, but worth a visit for the space-age lampshades alone. It's also a handy place to rest up, drink endless cups of coffee and chat to some down-to-earth locals at the lunch counter, should you tire of discussing Hans Wegner chairs around the corner on Beverly Boulevard.

470 N La Cienega Boulevard, T 323 654 8073, www.normsrestaurants.com

Seventh-Day Adventist Church

This is a true Los Angeles landmark in that it sits at the Hollywood Freeway and Hollywood Boulevard intersection, and is passed by hundreds of thousands of drivers every day. Its curved concrete form has been described as a 'boat of faith, riding a sea of humanity', or, more prosaically, as 'God's Own Gas Station'. The circle of steel fins from which the spire emerges is reminiscent of classic automotive design at the time of its early 1960s construction, so it is an appropriate cathedral for a car-obsessed city. Any visitor who stops will be rewarded inside by a nave covered by concrete planes held up by thin steel tubes. Between these planes, glass allows sequences of coloured light to wash over the interior.

1711 Van Ness Avenue, T 323 462 0010, www.hollywoodsda.org

Walt Disney Concert Hall

It has been described as a barge at full sail, a homage to the billowing skirts of Marilyn Monroe, a cubist masterpiece and the physical manifestation of a certain cartoon mouse's strokes with his magic wand. It is, in fact, dazzlingly beautiful, universally lauded and a home-town stainless steel victory for its designer Frank Gehry. Some say it surpasses the Guggenheim museum (T 00 34 94 435 9080) in Bilbao. After years of funding problems and delays, the project was almost killed off; it was designed in 1987 but failed to open until 2003. Now, it is the big, shiny hope of City fathers who pray that it will bring life back to moribund Downtown Los Angeles. If you get a chance, go to a concert – it's the home of the Los Angeles Philharmonic – if only to see the undulating beauty of the interior. *111 S Grand Avenue, T 323 850 2000, www.laphil.org*

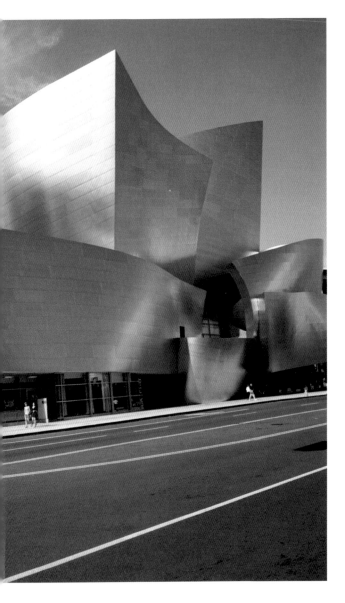

HOTELS

WHERE TO STAY AND WHICH ROOMS TO BOOK

With so many transient millionaires, it's hardly surprising that LA has always been famous for its hotels. But, in recent years, there have been so many chic new berths in town that they've made the city famous for design for the first time in decades. The people to thank for this include André Balazs and chief rival Brad Korzen, with help from his wife Kelly Wearstler.

André Balazs' mid-century-meets-gothic revamp kept Chateau Marmont (see p020) on top of the pile in the early 1990s. He then moved across Sunset Boulevard to create his once ice-cool, now lukewarm The Standard Hollywood (8300 Sunset Boulevard, T 323 650 9090) out of a former motel and retirement home. He followed this with The Standard Downtown (see p026), giving a sex-in-the-1970s feel to an old oil-company office block.

Then came Kelly and Brad, who took the Beverly Carlton Hotel and furnished the interior with pieces by Charles Eames, George Nelson and Eero Saarinen to produce Avalon (see p036). They've since made the tiny little Maison 140 (see p024), the Viceroy (see p028) and the Chamberlain (see p032) fit for those who like their hotels on the camp side. Meanwhile, the Morgans Hotel Group's all-white, hotel-as-theatre Mondrian (opposite) has managed to remain a hip hangout on the Strip for almost a decade, proving that it was more than just an in-joke.

For all addresses and room rates, see Resources.

Mondrian

It's almost a decade since it opened, but Schrager and Starck's box of tricks, with its glowing, surreal lobby populated, as it is, by eclectic furniture (above), is still a star of the Strip, and the Skybar remains popular, although the clientele may not be as beautiful as they once were – and they were very, very beautiful – but it's so dark in there you're never going to know. If you're bringing a white Mac laptop with

you, beware: if you put it down, you may lose it. The walls of the rooms are white, the carpet is white, so is the bed, and the chairs – you get the idea. The only safe place to put down your iBook is on top of the black TV, or you'll never find it again. The same goes for white underwear and very pale children.

8440 Sunset Boulevard, T 323 650 8999, www.mondrianhotel.com

The Pool, Mondrian

Chateau Marmont

This eccentric 1920s folly, perched above Sunset Boulevard, is still our first choice for digs in Los Angeles. The appeal of André Balazs' restored Chateau is not the fact that John Belushi's life ended here, but its private bungalows, lovely pool and lush gardens, overlooked by peaceful gothic-arched colonnades (above). And when you tire of these delights, you can settle into the comfortable lounge (left), furnished in traditional style, where things are low-key, celeb-packed but convivial compared to the multitudes crowding the Bar Marmont. Of course, there are hotels with better rooms and bigger pools, and someplace somewhere will be generating more buzz. But this is Chateau Marmont and there isn't anywhere else like it.

8221 Sunset Boulevard, T 323 656 1010, www.chateaumarmont.com

Maison 140

Obliging his esoteric tastes, Brad Korzen's Maison 140 stretches your imagination even further than Avalon (see p036), his first LA hotel. He hired interior designer Kelly Wearstler to go that extra mile – in fact, she went the distance and then some – creating interior spaces that walk a fine line between courageous and camp, but never fall into bad taste. She mixes 1920s styling and 1970s modernism with French and Asian influences, as seen in Bar Noir (left, T 310 407 7795). Walk into one of the 43 rooms from the all-black corridors and you're hit by a burst of pattern and colour. Choose from a smaller Parisian Room or a larger Mandarin Room (above), in a range of colour schemes, with custom-made beds and wallpaper.
140 S Lasky Drive, T 310 281 4000, www.maison140beverlyhills.com

The Standard Downtown
Far more successful than its precursor,
The Standard Hollywood (T 323 650
9090), this is definitely the place to stay
Downtown (if you have to). It's camp, but
in a good way (working it well in a macho
former oil-company HQ), with a fantastic
all-night retro-diner restaurant, stunning
Vladimir Kagan-designed lobby (right),
plus many luxurious rooms, including
the Huge Room with a bathtub (above)
and *The Man from U.N.C.L.E* fixtures and
fittings. No opportunity for a good
double entendre has been passed up: the
pencils have 'use me' written on them,
while each room's keycard has 'push me
in' as its instruction. The risqué joke gets
stretched pretty thin though: the room
phones include speed-dials for 'heaven',
'hell' and a 'fluffer' – perhaps more
Austin Powers than Illya Kuryakin.
550 S Flower Street/6th Street,
T 213 892 8080, www.standardhotel.com

Viceroy

Kelly Wearstler described Viceroy as 'modern with a colonial vibe', while *LA Times* design guru David A Keeps has identified it as a new, eclectic, 21st-century Hollywood style. Either way, it translates into yellow gentleman's-club furniture and matching 1970s-style carpets in the library (left), which also features eccentric modern shelves, and a mix of regency and contemporary style in the lobby (above).

The Whist restaurant, operated by executive chef, Warren Schwartz, has a strong reputation for its food and its A-list ambience. Its pool cabanas come with plasma screens, heaters, private waiters and an eye-popping $1,350 minimum spend if you want to reserve one for the chef's tasting night.
1819 Ocean Avenue, T 310 260 7500, www.viceroysantamonica.com

The Huntley Hotel

Thomas Schoos, who also designed West Hollywood restaurants Koi (T 310 659 9449) and Citizen Smith (see p057), chucked out a lot of chintz in his $12m revamp of The Huntley Hotel in 2005. Schoos has created a strangely tactile hotel, taking his inspiration from the nearby beach and Santa Monica's vaguely artsy reputation – which possibly explains the 220 white-lacquered ceramic piranhas that can be seen swimming along the walls of the lobby. The lounge is furnished with shag-pile carpets you could lose a small pony in. Meanwhile, the bedrooms are all decorated in a palette of earth tones, with luxurious suede headboards, as seen in this standard double with views of the Pacific (above), while the studio living rooms (right) include leather chairs and sumptuous lambswool rugs.
1111 2nd Street, T 310 394 5454, www.thehuntleyhotel.com

Chamberlain

A slightly more muted outpost of the Kor Hotel Group, the people behind Avalon (see p036) and Viceroy (see page 028), Chamberlain is all suites – even the smallest Studio Room (above) has a king-size bed and separate living area. The hotel also boasts a fantastic rooftop bar and pool, as well as an elegant bistro (right). It's handily situated for shopping on nearby Robertson Boulevard, its crowd has been described as 'young and design conscious', which could be a euphemism. Guests also have the unlimited use of a Sony PlayStation 2 or a PlayStation Portable device, free of charge. Should they find themselves having trouble with their shoot-'em-up games, they can call on the 'game butler' – another way in which the competition for guests is being played out at the upper end of LA's hotel scene.

1000 Westmount Drive, T 310 657 7400, www.chamberlainwesthollywood.com

The Beverly Hills Hotel and Bungalows
Since the 1920s, 'The Pink Palace', as it's known locally, has been the place where A-listers have felt free to frolic and you, too, can get nicely lost in the vast, lush tropical gardens and splendidly private walkways (left). If you have the resources, try one of the hotel's separate bungalows: Bungalow 3 (above) has its own entrance, kitchen and wood-burning stove, and many of the others have pianos, jacuzzis and treadmills. Even the rooms in the main hotel have three telephone lines each and televisions in their bathrooms. The Polo Lounge is still the place for major players to be with their own kind, while The Fountain Coffee Room (see p042) is a good place to see A-list divorced dads at weekend brunch with their children. *9641 Sunset Boulevard, T 310 276 2251, www.thebeverlyhillshotel.com*

Avalon

This is Kelly Wearstler's super-charming tribute to mid-century chic: it's all George Nelson lamps, Eames-ish chairs and Noguchi glass-topped tables. The Blue on Blue restaurant and bar, with its poolside curtained cabanas (above), draws a big crowd of the beautiful folk. When it opened, it was just about the hippest little spot in Beverly Hills, and it has maintained this cachet. Built from the bones of the old Beverly Carlton, once a hangout of Marilyn's, plus two adjoining apartment blocks, it was designed with an open-plan layout, so that some rooms open onto balconies overlooking the pool. Pea-green walls in some of the rooms mute the sub-*Jetsons* feel of the furnishings, and the whole thing is both fun and classy. *9400 W Olympic Boulevard, T 310 277 5221, www.avalonbeverlyhills.com*

Hollywood Roosevelt Hotel

The tried-and-tested, hotel-as-theatre strategy may have found its limits here. From its reopening in 2005, Roosevelt used young celebrities, parties, publicists and endless media coverage of its two nightspots, Teddy's and the Tropicana bar, to create an über-velvet-rope buzz about itself. It did this so well that non-celeb guests in the hotel started to complain about exclusion. Bar manager Amanda Scheer Demme, who got the stars in, soon parted company with the Thompson Hotels group (the people behind New York's 60 Thompson, T 1 877 431 0400). Still, despite the hype, the Dodd Mitchell-designed interiors, Cabana Suites (above) and pool bar make it a notable addition to the city's swish list.

7000 Hollywood Boulevard, T 323 466 7000, www.hollywoodroosevelt.com

Cabana Suite Patio,
Hollywood Roosevelt Hotel

24 HOURS

SEE THE BEST OF THE CITY IN JUST ONE DAY

The 'you drive everywhere' cliché about LA is so oft-repeated that it's easy to forget that once you get where you're going you will have to walk. Downtown, Santa Monica and Venice all contain perfectly strollable streets and, indeed, some of them, such as Santa Monica's 3rd, are even shut to cars, while the Venice Canals (see p043) and their surroundings can only be appreciated on foot. There are shops you'll need to amble past, like the hip perfumery Scent Bar (8327 Beverly Boulevard, T 323 782 8300), because otherwise they're so small you may miss them. Then there are places you'll want to go to on a whim, like Pho 97 (Suite 120, 727 N Broadway, T 213 625 7026), an unprepossessing noodle bar in a Chinatown strip mall, which aficionados believe might just serve the best Vietnamese street soup in North America.

You can walk the trails in Griffith Park or hike the unpaved western end of Mulholland Drive. Even parts of Sunset Boulevard should be walked, but with a landmark such as the cavernous music store Amoeba Music (6400 Sunset Boulevard, T 323 245 6400) as your focal point. All the same, to do the city justice in a day, you'll need to do some serious tarmac time. And to swoop from the mountains to the coast cities and then back to Downtown will take a street map, a hire car and a certain kind of Angelino reserve about your wine intake at lunch.

For all addresses, see Resources.

07.00 Mulholland Drive

To take in this curving and dramatic road, made famous by David Lynch, you'll need to get up before the traffic starts and after the Ferrari-racing rich kids have gone to bed. The road weaves along the top of LA's spine, swooping and twisting past modern SoCal (Southern Californian) homes, perched on the scrubby bluffs of the Santa Monica Mountains. You get great views over the city and, as you go west, the ocean cities. Then, as the road clips to the other side of the ridges, you get a glimpse of the great urban sprawl of the Valley. To get started, leave US 101 at the Barham Boulevard exit, cross the bridge over the highway, make a left back towards Hollywood and there will be a sign for Mulholland on your right.

08.00 The Fountain Coffee Room

The classic, over-the-top decor at this coffee shop in The Beverly Hills Hotel (see p034) is so bad, it's good. Something of an institution, with its curved, soda-fountain counter built in 1949, the place has been sympathetically restored. If you want to give in to a little golden-age-of-Hollywood nostalgia, this will be it. The café serves fresh-made pastries and the juice is squeezed after you order it, but that's hardly the point: The Fountain Coffee Room is simply a tiny, retro delight. In fact, it's so small, you won't find many other tourists there. But, you will find that there aren't many movie legends who haven't had breakfast where you're sitting.
9641 Sunset Boulevard, T 310 276 2251, www.thebeverlyhillshotel.com

10.30 The Venice Canals

Avoid the crowds, rollerblading loons and the buskers on the promenade at Venice Beach (see p090) and, instead, take a relaxed, morning stroll along the shady lanes and bridges around the canals at the southern end of Venice. Mr Abbot Kinney, who founded the town in 1904, envisioned a northern Italian cultural idyll on the West Coast and even brought over two dozen gondoliers from Europe to work on the canals. Originally, there were 23km of waterways, but much of it was paved over for the benefit of the cars, until the 1960s, when the likes of Jim Morrison started to move back and do up the properties. It's now one of the most desirable areas with a mix of residents from former hippies to business execs. *Between Washington Boulevard and Venice Boulevard*

13.00 Beacon

This Pan-Asian fusion restaurant has been a favourite hangout for LA's foodies since it opened. Despite Beacon being well off the beaten track, sited next to the former Helms Bakery Building and, even more shockingly, being relatively inexpensive, it's been hailed as the best Asian eaterie in town. In the kitchen is Kazuto Matsusaka, an LA superchef, who has worked at Spago (T 310 385 0880), where he had a hand in nurturing Californian cuisine, and at Chinois on Main (T 310 392 9025) in Santa Monica, where he helped to define fusion cooking for the city. After stints in Paris and New York, he has created that rare thing, an LA restaurant that's known for its cooking, rather than for the stars and schmoozers who go to eat there.
3280 Helms Avenue, T 310 838 7500, www.beacon-la.com

16.00 Ennis House

It's fair to say that Frank Lloyd Wright's 1924 exercise in domestic monumentalism has not aged well. Indeed, at one stage in 2005, after years of extensive earthquake and flood damage, it seemed certain the place would be condemned. Tours were called off because the Ennis House was deemed unsafe and it appeared on the list of 'America's 11 Most Endangered Historic Places', published annually by the National Trust for Historic Preservation. Happily, considerable progress has been made since then on restoring a building that single-handedly made concrete block construction respectable, and, of course, provided a suitably bleak, suitably futuristic set for Ridley Scott's 1982 cult science fiction classic *Blade Runner*.

2655 Glendower Avenue,
www.ennishouse.org

20.00 Noé Restaurant and Bar

At the top of the Omni Hotel (T 213 617 3300), the main attraction is British-born executive-chef Robert Gadsby's high-style presentation and progressive, complex combinations. His six and nine-course tasting menus are particularly inspiring, accompanied by Gadsby's own choice of drinks that are selected to bring out the top notes of each dish. Think minted mango frappé with a mimosa salad. The restaurant itself has two additional dining areas, which can be sealed off from the main dining area. Our favourite was the 18-seater Private Dining room with gold and cobalt-blue decor. There is also a patio, which overlooks the California Watercourt Plaza. Why not take a glass of something exclusive outside and drink in an equally exclusive Los Angeles skyline? No, we couldn't think why not either.

251 S Olive Street, T 213 356 4100,
www.noerestaurant.com

URBAN LIFE
CAFÉS, RESTAURANTS, BARS AND NIGHTCLUBS

Los Angeles is not a boozer's city. The long distances, the need to drive, the early-morning breakfast meetings; they all mean this is no Dublin or Prague. However, in terms of places to hang out, eye-up beautiful people and suck up some glamour, few cities can compete with Cahuenga Boulevard in Hollywood. Similarly, LA restaurant culture is not really about the food. With a few noble exceptions, the food will be decent, but it won't be challenging. Hollywood socialites go for salads, tuna tartare, New York strip steak, sushi, French-Asian fusion – in short, food that won't take any of the attention away from them. And Hollywood is where it's now at. Once run-down, the area is being reinvigorated by hot-spots owned by movie money, designed by the likes of Dodd Mitchell and hyped to the heavens by the celebs who grace their tables – usually because their agent has invested in the place. It's a formula, and one which often involves serving food until 4am.

Outside Hollywood things are slightly less precious – there are elegant dining choices in Santa Monica and funky options in Venice and Silver Lake. There is also the infamous American hamburger. Some argue about the merits of the 'In-N-Out burger' versus the 'Fatburger', but, for a real insider's junk food experience, try a 'Roscoe's House of Chicken 'n' Waffles' (1514 N Gower Street, T 323 466 7453) – and, yes, they do come on the same plate.
For all addresses, see Resources.

Republic Restaurant + Lounge

Restaurant row has a new star with Republic Restaurant + Lounge. Owner Mikayel Israyelyan enlisted designer Margaret O'Brien to set the stage – guests enter through the bar, past large leather sofas, python-upholstered bar, granite tops and glass-beaded wall finishes. The dining room houses a 20ft-tall wine tower, deer antler chandeliers and a huge cylinder fire pit shaded by stainless steel chain mail. The patio features sleek cabanas and giant parchment paper light fixtures by artist William Leslie. Executive chef Gabe Morales has created a contemporary American menu with a slightly Southern flair. Prime filet is thick as a brick and comes with a side of black truffle grits. *650 N La Cienega Boulevard, T 310 360 7070, www.therepublicla.com*

Geisha House
This seductive sushi bar and sake
lounge, part owned by actors Ashton
Kutcher and Sean Astin, is centred
around a red lacquer fireplace. Skilled
mixologists blend superior cocktails,
while master chef Genichi Mizoguchi
wows the crowd with miso black cod and
'Marilyn Monroll' with fresh crab.
6633 Hollywood Boulevard, T 323 460
6300, www.geishahousehollywood.com

The Otheroom
This micro-brewery and wine bar, which has sisters in New York and Miami, attracts the cool and the beautiful from across the Westside, so crowds and queues are common. The best way to avoid the line is to go with a Venice local, who'll get to the front if they have ID with a Venice address. Inside, it's a dark, industrial space with brick walls and a pressed-tin ceiling. The bar has an absolutely enormous selection of beers and wines – but no liquor licence, so don't come for a martini, and late on it can get very loud. The choice seats are by the high windows – perfect for eyeing up the passing street life.
1201 Abbot Kinney Boulevard, T 310 396 6230, www.theotheroom.com

Axe

With a sleek minimalist interior, Axe has a kind of Scandinavian Zen feeling to its bare concrete walls and benches. Axe is so minimalist, in fact, that the toilet doors have no irksomely cluttering, but useful, signage. It serves an eclectic mix of all-organic, farm-fresh Southern Californian cuisine, with Asian and Med influences, on big white plates. Think green tea and red coconut lamb curry. Also a cool place for a healthy salad during the day, it is often packed with the kind of Venice incomers who make the local hippies swear. Oh, and the name is pronounced *Ah-shay*, just in case you need to ask for directions. *1009 Abbot Kinney Boulevard, T 310 664 9787*

Falcon
Named after Rudolph Valentino's home, Falcon Lair, Falcon was part of the rebirth of Hollywood when it opened in 2002. It quickly became the gorgeous people's supper club, thanks to its heavy-duty velvet-rope policies and the usual LA ingredients: hot architects, a hot designer, and owners with pedigree. The food is hardly the point.
7213 Sunset Boulevard, T 323 850 5350

AOC

Many a local's favourite, AOC (which stands for Appellation d'Origine Contrôlée – a French certification that guarantees the origin and production standards of a wine) is the latest operation from Lucques (T 323 655 6277) duo, Suzanne Goin and Caroline Styne. Sort of a high-class wine-and-tapas bar, with crisp white tablecloths and brown leather sofas, it offers a choice of 50 excellent wines by the glass or carafe, a charcuterie bar and fantastic food in small, appetizer-sized portions. Goin's passion for locally-sourced, responsibly-farmed fresh ingredients complement Styne's handpicked choice of wines perfectly.

8022 W 3rd Street, T 323 653 6359, www.aocwinebar.com

Citizen Smith

Angelinos clearly believe that food eaten in the middle of the night won't make them fat. In late 2005 Citizen Smith joined Magnolia (T 323 467 0660), Honey (T 323 462 3000) and Memphis (T 323 465 8600) in offering the city's latest trend: supper served until well past midnight. Situated in the heart of the booming 'Cahuenga Corridor', Citizen Smith was designed by Thomas Schoos, who also designed Koi (T 310 659 9449), O-Bar (T 323 822 3300) and Wilshire (T 310 586 1707). He's given it bare brick walls, high ceilings hung with large cast iron chandeliers, lampshades printed with women's faces, and cowhide banquettes. It has three bars and serves food until 4am, including a *Seinfeld*-esque 'bottomless bowl of cereal'.
1602 N Cahuenga Boulevard,
T 323 461 5001

Patina

No world class cultural institute, from the Sydney Opera House (T 00 61 2 9250 7111) to the New York MoMA (T 00 1 212 708 9400), is complete without its own signature dining experience, so it was a coup for both building and restaurateur Joachim Splichal, when this renowned Melrose Avenue flagship transferred to the Walt Disney Concert Hall (see p014). It is now housed in one of the aluminium petals of Gehry's downtown landmark, and the restaurant's heaving and swelling ceiling and curvaceous booths reference the host structure. It has a great bar for pre-concert cocktails, and an outdoor patio for al fresco dining, but the real reason to come here is for the seafood or the $100 tasting menu. One of the best restaurants in the city, if not the country.
Walt Disney Concert Hall,
141 S Grand Avenue, T 213 972 3331,
www.patinagroup.com

Forty Deuce

When experienced Hollywood impresario Ivan Kane realised the lifespan on his namesake bar, Kane, was coming to an end after five years, he gutted it and turned it into a back-alley speakeasy. Now, complete with burlesque dancers (handpicked by Kane and his muse, Champagne Suzy), a three-piece jazz band, celebrity DJs and a kind of bump 'n' grind aesthetic, the place is a complete hoot and yet still draws a glittery crowd. In fact, the club has proved such a hit that branches are set to open in London, New York and San Diego.
5574 Melrose Avenue, T 323 466 6263, www.fortydeuce.com

CineSpace

A sharp looking restaurant and drinking space that serves great Cali cuisine and cocktails, but which really comes into its own on its signature 'Dinner & Movie' nights, when guests can sit back and enjoy free screenings of art-house films, cutting-edge movies and all-time classics while tucking into their Cineburger and fries (tables are set at an incline to allow decent views of the large screen).

If nothing takes your fancy on the playlist, visit their website in advance and request a movie to watch, or, better still, screen your own. As with any popular venue in LA, it gets crammed with gorgeous folk. A complete evening out in one place. *6356 Hollywood Boulevard, T 323 817 3456, www.cinespace.info*

Nacional
Travertine marble, ornamental railings
and cubist-inspired furniture may be
one explanation for the long lines and
A-list crowd that has been packing out
this Cuban-inspired club lounge for the
past few years. Or perhaps it's that the
management can create a buzz thanks
to well-exploited showbiz contacts and
an eye for great design.
1645 Wilcox Avenue, T 323 962 7712

Dresden Restaurant

Yes, the Dresden, in fashionable Los Feliz, is that bar from the film *Swingers*. And everyone knows it's that bar that featured in *Swingers*. But, hey, it's that bar from *Swingers* just like you thought it would be: cool. Lounge act Marty and Elayne haven't let film fame, or celebrity fans (Tom Petty featured them in one of his music videos) go to their heads. They celebrated 25 irony-free years of playing at the Dresden in 2006 and plan to go on for many years yet. The crowd is decidedly more arch than the music, but the bartenders' cosmopolitans are the real thing, and the white-leather decor makes for an authentic Golden Age ambience.
1760 N Vermont Avenue, T 323 665 4294, www.thedresden.com

The Brig

Emblematic of the change in Venice over the past few years is the story of ex-boxer Babe Brandelli's 58-year-old dive bar joint. Once much-loved by boho locals, it was bought out, refurbished and generally smartened up, much like the Venice strip it sits on. It now attracts a more shiny, well-heeled clientele, even if it did keep its pool table and mural of the famous Babe. The Brig has speckled terrazzo flooring, a huge stainless-steel bar and a retractable roof, designed by LA-based architects John Friedman and Alice Kimm. Order an apple martini and talk art and architecture with the new, refurbished local Venetians.
1515 Abbot Kinney Boulevard,
T 310 399 7537

The Brig

Vodbox
Faux-fur-clad guests are ushered by the vodka sommelier through the restaurant and bar and into a walk-in, drink-in, exhibition-style freezer, maintained at a frosty -12°C. Welcome to Vodbox, a stainless steel party cube, with vodka selections from the rare to the ridiculously obsolete.
453 N Canon Drive, T 310 550 5707, www.nicsbeverlyhills.com

INSIDER'S GUIDE

CHLOE BROOKMAN, ACCOUNT EXECUTIVE

Chloe Brookman is an account executive at Clifford PR in West Hollywood, whose clients include upscale hospitality designers ForrestPerkins and the Carolina Herrera label. She singles out Quality Food & Beverage (8030 W 3rd Street, T 323 658 5959) as one of the best-kept breakfast secrets in LA: 'They have the best biscuits, no lines, and are dog-friendly.' However, for a Sunday morning she recommends La Conversation (638 N Doheny Drive, T 310 858 0950), which serves delicious pastries and freshly-brewed coffee in a relaxed atmosphere (Havaianas and sweat pants are more than acceptable).

For a working lunch, Chloe recommends Orso (8706 W 3rd Street, T 310 274 7144), where the menu changes daily. For a quick lunch she plumps for the Casbah Café in Silver Lake (3900 W Sunset Boulevard, T 323 664 7000) – a good place for 'yummy dolmas and hummus, and a French-inspired menu'. The café also carries a line in unusual North African clothing, linens and curtains, and is a popular haunt for supermodels. For early evening drinks, she would go to Café Stella (3932 W Sunset Boulevard, T 323 666 0265) for its great wine menu and wonderful appetisers. For something a little more substantial, Chloe, an expat Brit, nominates Surya in West Hollywood (8048 W 3rd Street, T 323 653 5151) as one of the best places in town to source a chicken tikka masala.

ARCHITOUR

A GUIDE TO LA'S ICONIC BUILDINGS

As befits the city of the second chance, the built environment of Los Angeles has been constantly reinvented and reformulated, with a dizzying disregard for the past. Only a few poor adobe buildings date from the city's foundation, and then there's the Bradbury Building (304 S Broadway), one of the few notable 19th-century structures still standing. It was only after the First World War that the city began to expand and established its indiscriminately exotic (okay, chaotic) look. Everything from reinterpreted haciendas to beaux arts Egyptian tombs were put up. This was the period of Grauman's Chinese Theatre (6925 Hollywood Boulevard, T 323 464 8111) and the pyramid-topped art deco City Hall (200 N Spring Street).

No architour of LA could do the city justice without taking in the mid-century domestic buildings designed by Frank Lloyd Wright and his disciples, Richard Neutra, Rudolf M Schindler and John Lautner. Highlights include Wright's Ennis House (see p043), Schindler's Lovell Beach House (1242 W Ocean Front, Newport Beach, Orange County), and Neutra's Lovell Health House (4616 Dundee Drive). Lautner designed a wood-and-glass coffee shop called Googie's on Sunset Strip in 1949. Googie's gave its name to this futuristic style of architecture, which includes gems such as Norms Restaurant (see p012) in West Hollywood.

For all addresses, see Resources.

Cathedral of Our Lady of the Angels

This is the third largest cathedral in the world and, when work finished in 2002, it was the first Roman Catholic cathedral to have been built in the western US for over a quarter of a century. It is the work of celebrated Spanish architect José Rafael Moneo, who designed it so that, despite its bulk, it presents an understated aspect to the street, with a vast square hidden away behind the walls of the complex. It's only when you finally reach the cathedral, that the scale of the undertaking really becomes clear. You enter through a set of monumental bronze doors, which were designed by LA sculptor Robert Graham. These open onto a 70m walkway that runs the entire length of the cathedral from east to west.
555 W Temple Street, T 213 680 5200, www.olacathedral.org

LAX Theme Building

At one time, this quintessential LA symbol was the only architectural draw at the otherwise irredeemably dreary Los Angeles International Airport (LAX). Today, you can also see a spectacular series of light sculptures by Paul Tzanetopoulos, which almost make night-time arrivals fun. Built in 1960-61 by William Pereira, Luckman, Paul R Williams and Welton Becket to herald the arrival of the jet age, it doesn't seem to matter that the LAX Theme Building has become a type of visual shorthand for Los Angeles in a million movies and sitcoms. It doesn't matter that Walt Disney Imagineering refurbished the classic old restaurant within. What really matters most is that this landmark, in a city that's so devoted to reinvention, is a building that looks so unashamedly to the future.

1 World Way, T 310 646 5252, www.lawa.org

Getty Center Los Angeles

Perched 244m above sea level in the foothills of the Santa Monica Mountains, Richard Meier's Bauhaus-influenced, international-modernist building literally dazzles. With its 40,000 white-enamelled panels, travertine stone cladding and, most importantly, the bright LA light that flows in through its open-plan entrance and plazas, this is a museum for the kind of Angelinos who don't like to take off their sunglasses. The art galleries are illuminated by windows and skylights with computer-controlled louvres and a system of artificial lights programmed to respond to the season and time of day in order to maintain optimum natural light. The view from the southern end, over the LA basin, is one of the best in the city.

1200 Getty Center Drive, T 310 440 7300, www.getty.edu

Chemosphere

Julius Shulman's iconic photographs might have made this classic John Lautner building a bit too familiar for some, but there's no substitute for seeing first hand what an architect of genius could do with a tiny budget of $30,000, in a vertiginous mountainside location. The 45-degree slope imposed serious constraints, but apparently none at all to the architect's imagination. Restored by Frank Escher to something approaching its original state, it has become a symbol of 1960s optimism and also of today's mid-century real-estate mania. For a decade it had a 'For Sale' sign up and was parodied on *The Simpsons* as the mad, modern monstrosity they simply couldn't sell. These days, Lautner houses are owned by the likes of Courteney Cox Arquette and Vincent Gallo.
www.johnlautner.org

Salick Health Care Building

Beverly Boulevard is not, it should be said, best known for its architectural delights and, in any case, we'd usually think twice about steering you anywhere near a hospital, even one as justly renowned as the Cedars-Sinai Medical Center (T 310 423 3277). If you're going to make any trips to see health-care professionals on your travels though, it may as well be to admire their offices. This 1991 building shot Californian architectural practice Morphosis, founded by Thom Mayne, to international fame. It's actually a renovation of a 1960s building and is still used as a case study in teaching how to give new life to existing structures. The top-floor reception area offers fantastic views of West Hollywood and of northern Los Angeles.
8201 Beverly Boulevard, T 323 966 3400

SHOPPING

THE CITY'S BEST SHOPS AND WHAT TO BUY

As with anything in LA, the issue is of too much rather than too little. The highest density of clothes and interiors lies in a square of West Hollywood that runs from Robertson Boulevard in the east to La Brea Avenue in the west, and principally along Beverly Boulevard and Melrose Avenue. This is where you'll find everything from the ornate Hollywood Regency Phyllis Morris showroom, and her daughter's store 655 Home (both at 655 N Robertson Boulevard, T 310 289 6868/9), to Blackman Cruz (800 N La Cienega Boulevard, T 310 657 9228) and Jonathan Adler (8125 Melrose Avenue, T 323 658 8390). If you're in the design trade, some of the 130 showrooms in Cesar Pelli's Pacific Design Centre (8687 Melrose Avenue, T 310 657 0800) may just sell to you.

Moving east, Vermont Avenue, on the Los Feliz/Silver Lake borders, is full of shops and boutiques, including Show (1722 N Vermont Avenue, T 323 644 1960), for cutting-edge design, and Soap Plant/Wacko/La Luz de Jesus (4633 Hollywood Boulevard, T 323 663 0122), for kitsch collectables. Another enclave is Silver Lake Boulevard, near Effie Street, where Scott Mangan's Rubbish (1630 Silver Lake Boulevard, T 323 661 5575) was something of a trailblazer. Westside, on Main Street in Santa Monica, delights include Michele Sommerlath (1427 Abbot Kinney Boulevard, T 310 392 9905) and Obsolete (222 Main Street, T 310 399 0024). *For all addresses, see Resources.*

Surfing Cowboys

One of the shops that pre-date the rampaging gentrification of Abbot Kinney is Surfing Cowboys, a magical mix of interesting mid-century furniture and ephemera, high-quality vintage surf memorabilia – including a 1920s Tom Blake board that could be in a museum – skateboards and rare books. It's run by former fashion photographers Donna and Wayne Gunther, who decided to take the stuff they'd been collecting over the years and turn it into a business and a way of getting off the road. They're getting more interested in, and attracting interest for, their sinewy, 1960s California artisan one-off wooden pieces.
1624 Abbot Kinney Boulevard, T 310 450 4891, www.surfingcowboys.com

Equator Books
An Abbot Kinney anchor tenant, this gallery and bookstore specialises in out-of-print art and photography books, and topics such as street culture, LA lore and call girls. Its interior, designed by Iraqi-born Rania Alomar, is made up of layers of multi-ply to evoke numerous piles of paper and books.
1103 Abbot Kinney Boulevard, T 310 399 5544, www.equatorbooks.com

TableArt

Walter S Lowry and Stephen M Flynn chucked in their dull corporate jobs to open a shop devoted to fine dining and designer entertaining. The table settings change regularly, of course, and there is dinnerware, glassware, linens and also tableware from Meissen, Nymphenburg, KPM and Augarten, among others. Notables include their own line of two-tone lacquered salad bowls ($95), a pair of outré sterling-silver 'Leopard' candlesticks ($2,560) and Anthologie Quartett's 'Leave the Light On' porcelain cube, topped with a bronze matchstick ($125). You will see a lot of their lines in magazines, as the place is a honey trap for art designers and creative directors.
7977 Melrose Avenue, T 323 653 8278, www.tartontheweb.com

Little Tokyo Clayworks

A tiny shop pressed up against a lawyers' office on an unassuming Downtown street, a block east from the Caltrans Building (see p010), Little Tokyo Clayworks is an absolute must for collectors, and anyone who likes mid-century ceramics. Every piece of wall space in this blink-and-you'll-miss-it shop is crowded with unique vases and teapots — clay sculptures sit on lower shelves and in tiny, serene pebble gardens

in the window. Long-time owner Joanne Onaga has a great eye and carries unusual modern work by the likes of Rudy Fleck, Michael Frimkess and his wife and collaborator Magdalena Suarez.
106 Judge John Aiso Street, T 213 617 7193

Twentieth

Stefan Lawrence's 930 sq m of 20th-century design goes way beyond the usual suspects and includes, for instance, the complete Vladimir Kagan collection. The store is divided into two sections: one houses vintage furnishings and the other is a gallery showing the work of local modernist designers. A lot of Twentieth's business comes from film and television set designers looking for hip props to improve their characters' taste in design. New creations can range from Mickey Mouse models dipped in tar ($1,200) to Rothko-inspired lighting (from $2,000) and Jason Miller's lighting fixtures shaped like stag horns (from $250).
8057 Beverly Boulevard, T 323 904 1200, www.twentieth.net

Boom Studio

The huge HD Buttercup (T 310 558 8900) interiors warehouse at the junction of Helms Avenue and Venice Avenue in Culver City is home to a wide range of outlets, including recent start-up Floor Model, which sells Swedish and Danish mid-century pieces. In the same complex is Boom Studio (above), a perfectly formed retail outlet for Craig Varterian's modernist furniture, shelving and accessories. Previously, Boom supplied only speciality shops, interior design firms and children's stores. Toddlers will love his fibreglass 'Baby Ball' chairs ($170) and their parents the hexagonal 'Hive' shelf units ($100 per unit).

3239 Helms Avenue, T 310 202 1697, www.boomusa.com

SPORTS AND SPAS

WORK OUT, CHILL OUT OR JUST WATCH

Woody Allen was making jokes about LA's fitness fanaticism in the 1970s, and it hasn't got any less devout. Choices are dizzying, and subject to rapidly changing trends: first Bikram yoga, then boot camps (where the bourgeoisie pay to be treated like conscripts), and now iPods, which you can either leave at home (DJs spin decks 24 hours at various gyms), or bring along and download a workout soundtrack (www.itrain.com). There are gyms where you can get your car washed, too, such as 24 Hour Fitness (15301 Ventura Boulevard, T 818 728 6777), and gyms to be seen in, such as The Sports Club/LA (1835 Sepulveda Boulevard, T 310 473 1447) and Equinox (8590 W Sunset Boulevard, T 310 289 1900).

With no NFL team, and with ice hockey hard to take seriously in Southern California, baseball and basketball are the only major spectator sports. The LA Lakers, traditionally an expensive collection of egos, is the basketball team every other fan hates; but the city loves them, and tickets to see them at Staples Center (1111 S Figueroa Street, T 213 742 7340) are priced high. The LA Dodgers, whose 1958 move from Brooklyn is seen by some New York liberals as a seminal moment in sporting history, have a home in Dodger Stadium (1000 Elysian Park Avenue, T 323 224 2966), built illegally on the former Mexican community of Chavez Ravine, but the baseball has not been top flight for decades.

For all addresses, see Resources

Argyle Salon & Spa

For ludicrously luxurious pampering, it doesn't get much better than this. Housed in one part of the Sunset Tower Hotel (T 800 225 2637), formerly The Argyle, this 613 sq m, two-floor treatment centre offers side-by-side massages for couples, iPod plug-ins, plasma screens, space for bridal-shower spa outings, a white-marble Turkish hammam, scrubs, wraps and whatever-parts-you-want-waxing waxed.

Top-notch tonsorial guru Philip B is on hand, and you can get Botox and collagen injections, laser hair removal, or more traditional grooming in the form of a 45-minute shave (for $65), shoeshine and cigars. This is the kind of über-decadence the Romans were into just before the Barbarian hordes battered in their brains.
8358 Sunset Boulevard, T 323 623 9000, www.argylela.com

Venice Beach
Despite the tie-dyed tat and tattoo-tastic
feeling to the Venice boardwalk, it would
be a shame for any fit folk to come to LA
and not visit the ocean-front sports area,
better known as Muscle Beach. Begun in
1934 in neighbouring Santa Monica as a
government-funded training ground for
dancers, gymnasts, bodybuilders and
circus acts, Muscle Beach lays claim to
being the spark that ignited all modern
fitness trends. The site moved to Venice
in the 1960s, and continued to attract
the body beautiful and those who wish
to watch them. Today, as well as the
pumped-up displays of physical prowess,
the recreation zone offers basketball,
tennis, handball and volleyball – if you
feel like joining in, you can book a court
with the centre.
Venice Beach Recreation Center,
1800 Ocean Front Walk
T 310 399 2775, www.laparks.org

Dermalogica
Part treatment centre, part flagship
store, this 154 sq m centre offers
skincare ($60 for 45 minutes) in
show-stopping surroundings, which
are as cool as the brand's minimalist
packaging. Treatments are carried out
in 'pods' (right), each with its own music
and lighting to suit your mood. Try out
their new products at the Skin Bar.
1022 Montana Avenue, T 310 260 8682

The Rooftop

If the thought of the gym seems too much like hard work, head for the bar at the top of The Standard Downtown (see p026) for some poolside action instead. The bar is swathed in psychedelic AstroTurf and dotted with bright-red, space-age cabanas with vibrating waterbeds, which surround a sleek outdoor pool, while beautiful staff rustle up cocktails and appetisers for your post-swim refuel. At night, movies are projected onto the roof of a neighbouring building, but it's almost as entertaining to watch the traffic and eyewitness news helicopters as they track through the surrounding skyscrapers, giving the whole place a movie-set feel. On Sunday afternoons in summer this is *the* place for DJs, bar-scene celebs and pool partying – The Rooftop set off a craze for rooftop pools all over Downtown Los Angeles.
550 S Flower Street/6th Street,
T 213 892 8080, www.standardhotel.com

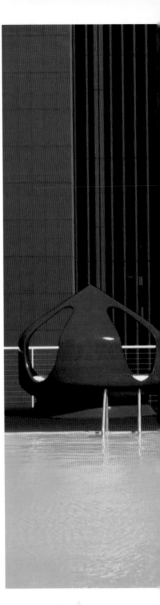

ESCAPES

WHERE TO GO IF YOU WANT TO LEAVE TOWN

What with being a sprawling mega-city and all, it's tempting to think that it takes long enough to cover LA county without going further afield, but the surrounding area has plenty to tempt you onto the freeways or commuter planes out of town. The most scenic route north is Highway 1, the Pacific Coast Highway, which will take you to Spanish-flavoured Santa Barbara, but if you have time, take a diversion to the idyllic town of Ojai (pronounced 'Oh-hi') at the foot of the Topa Topa mountains. North of Santa Barbara, those having a mid-life crisis may want to take Highway 101 to Buellton, in the Santa Ynez Valley, and the surrounding vineyard district to recreate their own *Sideways* fantasy trip.

To the north-east of LA, a long drive to Mojave and then US 395 and then Highway 190 will give you a breathtaking trip into the Death Valley National Park (www.nps.gov/deva). You can actually fly to Vegas, but it's more iconic to do it the *Swingers*/Gonzo way, driving overnight through the desert – just watch out for the giant bats near Barstow. Going south, you get to blandly pleasant San Diego. Although there are a number of ritzy towns, including La Jolla (La Hoy-a), on the way, the best way to get there is to take a 50-minute flight from LAX. From San Diego airport, hop over the border to Tijuana – for all the religious kitsch, nasty booze and cheap prescription drugs you might, or might not, want.

For all addresses, see Resources.

Parker Palm Springs

The first hotel by America's design darling Jonathan Adler was worth the wait. His maxim is that 'minimalism is a bummer', so it came as little surprise that, when he was commissioned to transform Palm Springs' former Givenchy Resort Spa, once owned by 1970s talk-show host Merv Griffin, he decided on a 'happy luxe' design philosophy, focusing on comfort and colour. Picture a lounge with a suit of armour ruling over a mix of contemporary and retro furniture and you get the idea. Each of the 131 bedrooms and 12 one-bedroom villas are slightly different, but for a really special treat, opt for the two-bedroom Gene Autry Residence, which Adler describes as 'super-luxe' digs.
4200 East Palm Canyon Drive, Palm Springs, T 1760 770 5000, www.theparkerpalmsprings.com

Rear Lounge, Parker Palm Springs

Viceroy Palm Springs

It wasn't just Sonny Bono who rescued this desert playground from its reputation as 'God's Waiting Room (With Golf Attached)'. The growth of interest in the town's glut of mid-century architecture, combined with a thriving gay community, has helped to put the Springs firmly back on the high-end traveller's map. But it was only really the opening of a slew of design-led hotels that helped complete this transformation, led by Kelly Wearstler's revamped Viceroy Palm Springs (T 1 760 320 4117, below) and the Parker Palm Springs (see p097). Both share a disdain for the kind of antiseptic minimalism of designer hotels of the recent past. And while Wearstler's eclectic mix of vibrant patterns and organic furnishings usually makes for the most rococo offering in town, here her hotel seems almost staid next to the Parker. The hotel's splendid, over-the-top pool (right) helps restore the glamour quotient.

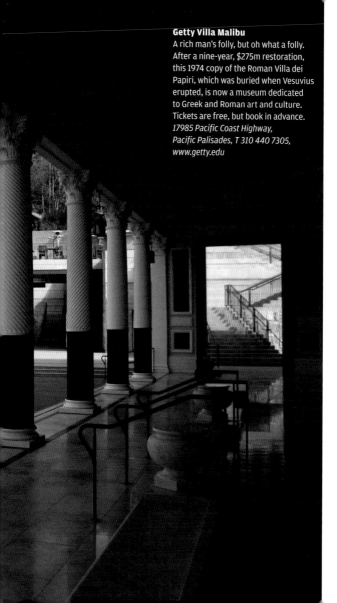

Getty Villa Malibu
A rich man's folly, but oh what a folly.
After a nine-year, $275m restoration,
this 1974 copy of the Roman Villa dei
Papiri, which was buried when Vesuvius
erupted, is now a museum dedicated
to Greek and Roman art and culture.
Tickets are free, but book in advance.
17985 Pacific Coast Highway,
Pacific Palisades, T 310 440 7305,
www.getty.edu

NOTES

SKETCHES AND MEMOS

RESOURCES

ADDRESSES AND ROOM RATES

LANDMARKS

010 MOCA
250 S Grand Avenue
T 213 626 6222
www.moca.org

**010 Caltrans District 7
Headquarters**
100 S Main Street

012 Norms Restaurant
470 N La Cienega Boulevard
T 323 654 8073
www.normsrestaurants.com

012 Pann's
6710 LaTijera Boulevard
www.panns.com
T 310 670 1441

**013 Seventh-Day
Adventist Church**
1711 N Van Ness Avenue
T 323 462 0010
www.hollywoodsda.org

**014 Walt Disney
Concert Hall**
11 S Grand Avenue
T 323 850 2000
www.laphil.org

014 Guggenheim Bilbao
Abandoibarra Et 2
Bilbao
Spain
T 00 34 94 435 9080
*www.guggenheim-
bilbao.es*

HOTELS

**016 The Standard
Hollywood**
Room rates:
double, $175
8300 Sunset Boulevard
T 323 650 9090
www.standardhotel.com

017 Mondrian
Room rates:
double, $335
8440 Sunset Boulevard
T 323 650 8999
www.mondrianhotel.com

020 Chateau Marmont
Room rates:
double, $335
8221 Sunset Boulevard
T 323 656 1010
www.chateaumarmont.com

024 Maison 140
Room rates:
double, $209;
Mandarin Rooms, $269;
Parisian Rooms, $239
140 S Lasky Drive
T 310 281 4000
www.maison140
beverlyhills.com

024 Bar Noir
Maison 140
140 S Lasky Drive
T 310 407 7795
www.maison140
beverlyhills.com

**026 The Standard
Downtown**
Room rates:
double, $150;
Huge Room, $205
*550 S Flower Street/
6th Street*
T 213 892 8080
www.standardhotel.com

028 Viceroy
Room rates:
double, $319
1819 Ocean Avenue
T 310 260 7500
www.viceroysantamonica.com

030 The Huntley Hotel
Room rates:
double, $369;
studio, $550
1111 2nd Street
T 310 394 5454
www.thehuntleyhotel.com

030 Koi
730 N La Cienega Boulevard
T 310 659 9449
www.koirestaurant.com

032 Chamberlain
Room rates:
double, $270;
Studio Room, $240
1000 Westmount Drive
T 310 657 7400
*www.chamberlain
westhollywood.com*

034 The Beverly Hills Hotel and Bungalows
Room rates:
double, $440;
Bungalow 3, $2,400
9641 Sunset Boulevard
T 310 276 2251
www.thebeverly
hillshotel.com

036 Avalon
Room rates:
double, $289
9400 W Olympic Boulevard
T 310 277 5221
www.avalonbeverly
hills.com

037 Hollywood Roosevelt Hotel
Room rates:
double, $245;
Cabana Suite, $1,500
7000 Hollywood Boulevard
T 323 466 7000
www.hollywood
roosevelt.com

037 60 Thompson
Room rates:
double, $545
60 Thompson Street
New York
T 1 877 431 0400
www.60thompson.com

24 HOURS
040 Amoeba Music
6400 Sunset Boulevard
T 323 245 6400
www.amoebamusic.com

040 Pho 97
Suite 120
727 N Broadway
T 213 625 7026

040 Scent Bar
8327 Beverly Boulevard
T 323 782 8300
www.luckyscent.com

042 The Fountain Coffee Room
The Beverly Hills Hotel and Bungalows
9641 Sunset Boulevard
T 310 276 2251
www.thebeverly
hillshotel.com

045 Venice Canals
Between Washington Boulevard and Venice Boulevard

044 Beacon
3280 Helms Avenue
T 310 838 7500
www.beacon-la.com

044 Chinois on Main
2709 Main Street
T 310 329 9025

044 Spago
176 N Canon Drive
T 310 385 0880

045 Ennis House
2655 Glendower Avenue
www.ennishouse.org

046 Noé Restaurant and Bar
Omni Hotel
251 S Olive Street
T 213 356 4100
www.noerestaurant.com

046 Omni Hotel
251 S Olive Street
T 213 617 3300
www.omnihotels.com

URBAN LIFE
048 In-N-Out
www.in-n-out.com

048 Fatburger
www.fatburger.net

048 Roscoe's House of Chicken 'n' Waffles
1514 N Gower Street
T 323 466 7453
www.roscoeschicken
andwaffles.com

049 Republic Restaurant + Lounge
650 N La Cienega Boulevard
T 310 360 7070
www.therepublicla.com

050 Geisha House
6633 Hollywood Boulevard
T 323 460 6300
www.geishahouse
hollywood.com

052 The Otheroom
1201 Abbot Kinney
Boulevard
T 310 396 6230
www.theotheroom.com

053 Axe
1009 Abbot Kinney
Boulevard
T 310 664 9787

054 Falcon
7213 Sunset Boulevard
T 323 850 5350

056 AOC
8022 W 3rd Street
T 323 653 6359
www.aocwinebar.com

056 Lucques
8474 Melrose Avenue
T 323 655 6277
www.lucques.com

057 Citizen Smith
1602 N Cahuenga
Boulevard
T 323 461 5001

057 Honey
1733 N Vine Street
T 323 462 3000

057 Magnolia
6266 W Sunset Boulevard
T 323 467 0660

057 Memphis
6541 Hollywood Boulevard
T 323 465 8600

057 O-Bar
8279 Santa Monica
Boulevard
T 323 822 3300
www.obarrestaurant.com

057 Wilshire
2454 Wilshire Boulevard
T 310 586 1707
www.wilshire
restaurant.com

058 Patina
Walt Disney Concert Hall
141 S Grand Avenue
T 213 972 3331
www.patinagroup.com

058 Sydney Opera House
T 0061 2925 07111
www.sydneyopera
house.com

058 MoMA
11 W 53rd Street
New York
T 1 212 708 9400
www.moma.org

060 Forty Deuce
5574 Melrose Avenue
T 323 466 6263
www.fortydeuce.com

061 CineSpace
6356 Hollywood Boulevard
T 323 817 3456
www.cinespace.info

062 Nacional
1645 Wilcox Avenue
T 323 962 7712

064 Dresden Restaurant
1760 N Vermont Avenue
T 323 665 4294
www.thedresden.com

065 The Brig
1515 Abbot Kinney
Boulevard
T 310 399 7537

068 Vodbox
Nic's Martini Lounge
453 N Canon Drive
T 310 550 5707
www.nicsbeverlyhills.com

**070 Quality Food
& Beverage**
8030 W 3rd Street
T 323 658 5959

070 La Conversation
638 N Doheny Drive
T 310 858 0950

070 Orso
8706 W 3rd Street
T 310 274 7144
www.orsorestaurant.com

070 Casbah Café
3900 W Sunset Boulevard
T 323 664 7000

070 Café Stella
3932 W Sunset Boulevard
T 323 666 0265

070 Surya
8048 W 3rd Street
T 323 653 5151

ARCHITOUR
072 Bradbury Building
304 S Broadway
072 City Hall
200 N Spring Street
**072 Grauman's
Chinese Theatre**
6925 Hollywood Boulevard
T 323 464 8111

SPORTS AND SPAS

088 Dodgers Stadium
1000 Elysian Park Avenue
T 323 224 2966
www.dodgers.com
088 Equinox
8590 Sunset Boulevard
T 310 289 1900
www.equinoxfitness.com
088 24 Hour Fitness
Sherman Oaks Galleria Club
15301 Ventura Boulevard
T 818 728 6777
www.24hourfitness.com
088 The Sports Club / LA
1835 Sepulveda Boulevard
T 310 473 1447
www.thesportsclubla.com
088 Staples Center
1111 S Figueroa Street
T 213 742 7340
www.staplescenter.com
**089 Argyle Salon
& Spa**
Sunset Tower Hotel
8358 Sunset Boulevard
T 310 623 9000
www.argylela.com
089 Sunset Tower Hotel
8358 Sunset Boulevard
T 800 225 2637
*www.sunsettower
hotel.com*
**090 Venice Beach
Recreation Center**
1800 Ocean Front Walk
T 310 399 2775
www.laparks.org

092 Dermalogica
1022 Montana Avenue
T 310 260 8682
094 The Rooftop
The Standard Downtown
*550 S Flower Street/
6th Street*
T 213 892 8080
www.standardhotel.com

ESCAPES

097 Parker Palm Springs
*4200 East Palm
Canyon Drive*
Palm Springs
T 1 760 770 5000
*www.theparkerpalm
springs.com*
**100 Viceroy
Palm Springs**
415 South Belardo Road
Palm Springs
T 1 760 320 4117
*www.viceroypalm
springs.com*
**102 Getty
Villa Malibu**
*17985 Pacific
Coast Highway*
Pacific Palisades
T 310 440 7305
www.getty.edu

WALLPAPER* CITY GUIDES

Editorial Director
Richard Cook

Art Director
Loran Stosskopf
City Editor
Paul McCann
Project Editor
Rachael Moloney
Series Editor
Jeroen Bergmans
Executive Managing Editor
Jessica Firmin

Chief Designer
Ben Blossom
Designers
Dominic Bell
Sara Martin
Ingvild Sandal
Map Illustrator
Russell Bell

Photography Editor
Emma Blau
Photography Assistant
Jasmine Labeau

Sub-Editor
Paul Sentobe
Editorial Assistant
Milly Nolan

Wallpaper* Group Editor-in-Chief
Jeremy Langmead
Creative Director
Tony Chambers
Publishing Director
Fiona Dent

Thanks to
Paul Barnes
Alicia Foley
David McKendrick
Claudia Perin
Meirion Pritchard
James Reid

PHAIDON

Phaidon Press Limited
Regent's Wharf
All Saints Street
London N1 9PA

Phaidon Press Inc
180 Varick Street
New York, NY 10014

www.phaidon.com

First published 2006
© 2006 Phaidon Press
Limited

ISBN 0 7148 4688 0

A CIP Catalogue record for
this book is available from
the British Library.

All prices are correct at
time of going to press, but
are subject to change.

Printed in China

PHOTOGRAPHERS

Benny Chan, Fotoworks
Falcon, pp054-055
The Brig, p065,
pp066-p067

Aaron Cook
AOC, p056

Roger Davies
Caltrans District
7 Headquarters,
pp010-011
Norms Restaurant, p012
Seventh-Day Adventist
Church, p013
Mulholland Drive, p041
Beacon, p044
The Otheroom, p052
Nacional, pp062-063
Dresden Restaurant, p064
Chloe Brookman, p071
Surfing Cowboys, p081
Equator Books, pp082-83
TableArt, p084
Little Tokyo Clayworks,
p085
Twentieth, p086
Boom Studio, p087

Denis Freppel
Chemosphere, p078
Salick Health Care
Building, p079

Saam Gabby
Axe, p053

**Chad Ehlers, Rex
Features**
Los Angeles City View,
inside front cover

**Bradley Johnson,
Machado and Silvetti
Associates**
Getty Villa Malibu,
pp102-103

Jeremy Samuelson
Parker Palm Springs,
p097, pp098-099

Laura Swimmer
Cathedral of Our Lady of
the Angels, p073

Alex Vertikoff
Getty Center Los Angeles,
pp076-077

Laura Wilson
Walt Disney Concert Hall,
pp014-015
Venice Canals, p043
Ennis House, p045
LAX Theme Building,
pp074-075
Venice Beach, pp090-091

LOS ANGELES
A COLOUR-CODED GUIDE TO THE CITY'S HOT 'HOODS

WEST HOLLYWOOD AND MIDTOWN
Home to LA's gay community and, not coincidentally, where you'll find sumptuous shops

SANTA MONICA, VENICE AND CULVER CITY
The three neighbouring cities are at different levels of development, but are all on the up

HOLLYWOOD
Avoid the tourist tat of the Boulevard and check out the area's slick bars and clubs

LOS FELIZ, SILVER LAKE AND ECHO PARK
Cool, very cool. There's more Neutra here than you'll know what to do with

WESTWOOD AND BEVERLY HILLS
Characterless but still unmissable, thanks to the sprinkling of industry magic throughout

DOWNTOWN
Not a nice place to linger, but not the no-go zone of old. MOCA is worth the trip alone

For a full description of each neighbourhood,
including the places you really must not miss, see the Introduction